SNOW,
GLASS,
APPLES™

SNOW, GLASS, APPLES™

Stories & Words
NEIL GAIMAN

Adaptation & Art
COLLEEN DORAN

HEADLINE

With respect and gratitude, the artist wishes to acknowledge her debt to
HARRY CLARKE
(Irish artist)
1889–1931

With colour flatting assistance from
VAL TRULLINGER

SNOW, GLASS, APPLES © & ™ 2019 Neil Gaiman
Artwork copyright © 2019 Colleen Doran

Names: Gaiman, Neil, author. | Doran, Colleen, 1963- artist.

Title: Snow, Glass, Apples / Neil Gaiman, stories and words; Colleen Doran, adaptation and art.

First published in the US in 2019 by Dark Horse Books
A division of Dark Horse Comics LLC

First published in Great Britain in 2019 by
HEADLINE PUBLISHING GROUP

1

Designer: Cindy Cacerez-Sprague

Cataloguing in Publication Data is available from the British Library

ISBN 978 1 4722 6291 2

Printed and bound in Italy by Lego SpA

Headline's policy is to use papers that are natural, renewable and recyclable
products and made from wood grown in sustainable forests. The logging
and manufacturing processes are expected to conform to the environmental
regulations of the country of origin.

HEADLINE PUBLISHING GROUP
An Hachette UK Company
Carmelite House
50 Victoria Embankment
London EC4Y 0DZ

www.headline.co.uk
www.hachette.co.uk

I do not know what manner of thing she is. None of us do. She killed her mother in the birthing, but that's never enough to account for it.

They call me wise, but I am far from wise, for all that I foresaw fragments of it, frozen moments caught in pools of water...

...or in the cold glass of my mirror.

If I were wise I would not have tried to change what I saw. If I were wise I would have killed myself before ever I encountered her, before ever I caught him.

Wise, and a witch, or so they said, and I'd seen his face in my dreams and in reflections for all my life: sixteen years of dreaming of him before he reined his horse by the bridge that morning and asked my name.

He helped me onto his high horse and we rode together to my little cottage, my face buried in the gold of his hair.

His daughter was only a child: no more than five years of age when I came to the palace.

A portrait of her dead mother hung in the princess's tower room: a tall woman, hair the color of dark wood, eyes nut-brown.

She was of different blood to her pale daughter.

The girl would not eat with us.

I do not know where in the palace she ate.

I had my own chambers. My husband the king, he had his own rooms also.

When he wanted me he would send for me, and I would go to him, and pleasure him, and take my pleasure with him.

One night, several months after I was brought to the palace, she came to my rooms.

She was six. I was embroidering by lamplight, squinting my eyes against the lamp's smoke and fitful illumination.

She looked up at me and smiled. Her teeth seemed sharp, even then, in the lamplight.

She said nothing. Her eyes were black as coal, black as her hair—her lips were redder than blood.

PRINCESS?

WHAT ARE YOU DOING AWAY FROM YOUR ROOM?

I'M HUNGRY.

It was winter, when fresh food is a dream of warmth and sunlight—but I had strings of whole apples, cored and dried, hanging from the beams of my chamber.

The next day it was an old scar: I might have cut my hand with a pocketknife in my childhood.

I had been frozen by her, owned and dominated. That scared me, more than the blood she had fed on.

After that night I locked my chamber door at dusk, barring it with an oaken pole—

—and I had the smith forge iron bars, which he placed across my windows.

My husband, my love, my king, sent for me less and less—

They say I was fooled—that it was not her heart. That it was the heart of an animal—a stag, perhaps, or a boar.

They say that, and they are wrong.

And some say (but it is her lie, not mine) that I was given the heart, and that I ate it.

Lies and half-truths fall like snow, covering the things that I remember, the things I saw. A landscape, unrecognizable after a snowfall—that is what she has made of my life.

There were scars on my love, her father's, thighs, and on his ballock-pouch, and on his male member, when he died.

I did not go with them. They took her in the day, while she slept and was at her weakest.

The forest is a dark place, the border to many kingdoms—no one would be foolish enough to claim jurisdiction over it.

Outlaws live in the forest. Robbers live in the forest, and so do wolves.

They took her to the heart of the forest, and there they opened her blouse.

You can ride through the forest for a dozen days and never see a soul...

They cut out her heart, and they left her dead, in a gully, for the forest to swallow.

...but there are eyes upon you the entire time.

They brought me her heart. I know it was—no sow's heart or doe's would have continued to beat and pulse after it had been cut out, as that one did.

I took it to my chamber...I did not eat it.

The stallholders at the fair were afraid of the forest folk.

They would nail their wares to the bare boards of their stalls—slabs of gingerbread or leather belts were nailed with great iron nails to the wood.

If their wares were not nailed, they said, the forest folk would take them, and run away, chewing on the stolen gingerbread, flailing about them with the belts.

The forest folk had money, though: a coin here, another there, sometimes stained green by time or the earth, the face on the coin unknown to even the oldest of us.

Also they had things to trade, and thus the fair continued, serving the outcasts and the dwarfs, serving the robbers (if they were circumspect) who preyed on the rare travelers from lands beyond the forest, or on gypsies, or on the deer.

This was robbery in the eyes of the law. The deer were the queen's.

The years passed by slowly, and my people claimed that I ruled them with wisdom.

The heart still hung above my bed, pulsing gently in the night.

If there were any who mourned the child, I saw no evidence.

She was a thing of terror, back then, and they believed themselves well rid of her.

Spring Fair followed Spring Fair.

Five of them, each sadder, poorer, shoddier than the one before. Fewer of the forest folk came out of the forest to buy.

Those who did seemed subdued and listless. The stallholders stopped nailing their wares to the boards of their stalls.

And by the fifth year but a handful of folk came from the forest—a fearful huddle of little hairy men, and no one else.

The Lord of the Fair, and his page, came to me when the fair was done. I had known him slightly, before I was queen.

I DO NOT COME TO YOU AS MY QUEEN.

I said nothing. I listened.

She was no longer a little child.

Her skin was still pale, her eyes and hair coal-black, her lips as red as blood.

She wore the clothes she had worn when she left the castle for the last time—the blouse, the skirt—although they were much let-out, much mended.

Over them she wore a leather cloak, and instead of boots she had leather bags, tied with thongs, over her tiny feet.

She was standing in the forest, beside a tree.

As I watched, in the eye of my mind, I saw her edge and step and flitter and pad from tree to tree, like an animal: a bat or a wolf.

She was following someone.

He was a monk. He wore sackcloth, and his feet were bare, and scabbed and hard.

His beard and tonsure were of a length, overgrown, unshaven.

She watched him from behind the trees.

Eventually he paused for the night, and began to make a fire—

—laying twigs down, breaking up a robin's nest as kindling.

There had been two eggs in the nest he had found—

—and these he ate raw. They cannot have been much of a meal for so big a man.

Naked, I was, and alone in the highest tower of the palace, a place open to the sky.

The winds chilled my body—goose pimples crept across my arms and thighs and breasts.

I carried a silver basin, and a basket in which I had placed a silver knife, a silver pin, some tongs, a gray robe and three green apples.

I put them on and stood there, unclothed, on the tower, humble before the night sky and the wind.

Had any man seen me standing there, I would have had his eyes—but there was no one to spy.

Clouds scudded across the sky, hiding and uncovering the waning moon.

I took the silver knife and slashed my right arm—once, twice, three times.

The blood dripped into the basin, scarlet seeming black in the moonlight.

When dawn began to brighten the sky, I covered myself with the gray cloak, and took the red apples from the silver bowl.

I lifted each into my basket with silver tongs, taking care not to touch it. There was nothing left of my blood or of the brown powder in the silver bowl, nothing save a black residue, like verdigris, on the inside.

I buried the bowl in the earth.

Then I cast a glamour on the apples...

...(as once, years before, by a bridge, I had cast a glamour on myself)...

...that they were, beyond any doubt, the most wonderful apples in the world—and the crimson blush of their skins was the warm color of fresh blood.

I pulled the hood of my cloak low over my face. I took ribbons and pretty hair ornaments with me, placed them above the apples in the reed basket.

I walked alone into the forest, until I came to her dwelling: a high sandstone cliff, laced with deep caves going back a way into the rock wall.

There were trees and boulders around the cliff face, and I walked quietly and gently from tree to tree, without disturbing a twig or a fallen leaf.

Eventually I found my place to hide, and I waited, and I watched.

After some hours, a clutch of dwarfs crawled out of the cave-front—ugly, misshapen, hairy little men, the old inhabitants of this country.

You saw them seldom now.

They vanished into the wood, and none of them espied me, though one of them stopped to piss against the rock I hid behind.

I waited. No more came out.

I went to the cave entrance and hallooed into it, in a cracked old voice.

The scar on my Mound of Venus throbbed and pulsed as she came towards me, out of the darkness, naked and alone.

By the time I reached my chambers, the heart that hung from the roof beam, with the apples and hams and the dried sausages, had ceased to beat.

It hung there, quietly, without motion or life, and I felt safe once more.

That winter the snows were high and deep, and were late melting.

We were all hungry come the spring.

The Spring Fair was slightly improved that year.

The forest folk were few, but they were there, and there were travelers from the lands beyond the forest.

I saw the little hairy men of the forest cave buying and bargaining for pieces of glass, and lumps of crystal and of quartz rock.

They paid for the glass with silver coins—the spoils of my stepdaughter's depredations, I had no doubt.

When it got about what they were buying, townsfolk rushed back to their homes and came back with their lucky crystals, and, in a few cases, with whole sheets of glass.

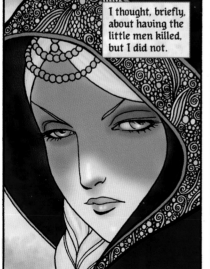

I thought, briefly, about having the little men killed, but I did not.

As long as the heart hung, silent and immobile and cold, from the beam of my chamber, I was safe, and so were the folk of the forest, and thus, eventually, the folk of the town.

My twenty-fifth year came, and my stepdaughter had eaten the poisoned fruit two winters back, when the prince came to my palace.

He was tall, very tall, with cold green eyes and the swarthy skin of those from beyond the mountains.

He rode with a small retinue: large enough to defend him, small enough that another monarch—myself, for instance—would not view him as a potential threat.

She pulled down the twine on which her heart was hanging.

She pulled off the dried rowan berries, one by one; pulled off the garlic bulb—now a dried thing, after all these years; then she took up her own, her pumping heart—

A small thing, no larger than that of a nanny goat or a she-bear—as it brimmed and pumped its blood into her hand.

Her finger-nails must have been as sharp as glass.

She opened her breast with them, running them over the purple scar.

Her chest gaped, suddenly, open and bloodless.

She licked her heart, once, as the blood ran over her hands.

And she pushed the heart deep into her breast.

It is starting to get hot in here.

They have told the people bad things about me—a little truth to add savor to the dish, but mixed with many lies.

I was bound and kept in a tiny stone cell beneath the palace, and I remained there through the autumn.

Today they fetched me out of the cell.

They stripped the rags from me, and washed the filth from me, and then they shaved my head and my loins, and they rubbed my skin with goose grease.

The snow was falling as they carried me—two men at each hand, two men at each leg—utterly exposed, and spread-eagled and cold, through the midwinter crowds; and brought me to this kiln.

My stepdaughter stood there with her prince.

She watched me, in my indignity, but she said nothing.

I will not
scream.

I will not give them
the satisfaction.

They will have my body, but my
soul and my story are my own,
and will die with me.

The goose-grease
begins to melt and
glisten upon my
skin. I shall make
no sound at all. I
shall think no
more on this.

I shall think
instead of the
snowflake on
her cheek.

SNOW, GLASS, APPLES™

Notes by
COLLEEN DORAN

I've admired Harry Clarke's work since I was a teenager. I mistook his drawing *An Angel of Peace* for art by Aubrey Beardsley, then spent years trying to track down information about his life and creations. He became a major influence on my work, but there wasn't much enthusiasm for this highly decorative style when I first got into comics, so I didn't get much opportunity to go as far as I wanted with this look.

Neil Gaiman, also a great admirer of Clarke, decided that *Snow, Glass, Apples* would be a great story for this style.

Here you see early cover designs and sketches. I wish I'd been able to complete that second sketch as well as the final! Maybe I'll finish it later, just for kicks.

Page # 2

Page # 1

To the right, another unused cover sketch, which Neil wisely decided looked too much like a young-adult novel. We didn't want this book to appeal to kids, for obvious reasons.

On this page, scans of the art in progress. Most of the art on this book was done entirely by hand, including all the niggling little details and heavy blacks. As you may imagine, this is an exceptionally labour-intensive approach.

The kitchen scene was one of my favourites to draw. My colouring assistant Val Trullinger, with whom I worked on *Amazing Fantastic Incredible Stan Lee*, ended up doing much of the colour on this page. However, I decided it would be safest to have Val help out with flats but do the rest of the final colour myself because it was too hard to match colouring styles. I ended up repainting everything, even my own flats, which I'd botched at one point. Since this is my first major project colouring line art, and I'd never worked with a flatter before, her technical assistance was a huge help.

The erotic scenes were a bit of a challenge, as I struggled with how far to take the material.

I really enjoyed doing the opening double-page spread with the young queen and her king. It turned out more nouveau and less Harry Clarke than I intended, though.

I spent more time redoing art on this book than on anything I've ever drawn before, with nearly half my drawings thrown out after I began inking.

I don't do tight pencils when I ink my own work. But on this art, the final inks had to be so precise and clean that there just wasn't much wiggle room. When I made a mistake, I felt compelled to redo the whole page.

As the deadline marched on, this was a luxury I couldn't afford, as my editor can attest.

I did three versions of this page as Snow White confronts the queen. I took my original sketches, scanned them, then cut and pasted elements on the computer to work out the final composition.

The manga-looking eyes you see here are based on Clarke's style.

Over the years people assume I adopted this look into my comic art from manga, but the *fin de siècle*-era artists, creators like Beardsley and Clarke, were my early influences long before I'd ever seen manga. Clarke's work predates the manga big-eye affectation, though I'm sure I was predisposed to liking manga art because of my exposure to Beardsley and Clarke.

Clarke's approach to the human figure is very attenuated and affected, and I didn't want it to dominate the feel of the book. Still, I went with a more stylised look than I usually do.

I strictly limited panel borders and used page flow to indicate the passage of time, mood, and feeling. For moments that require time beats, as on page 48, I used panel borders.

Most of the story is told from inside the queen's head, so I wanted a free-flowing sensibility. The challenge is to keep the narrative moving without confusing the reader or the poor letterer, who needs to be very careful with his word balloon placement.

For final pencils, I scanned the thumbnails, which are only about two inches high, blew them up to the final page size of about 9″ x 13″, and using a lightbox, traced the thumbnails onto a sheet of Bristol board. This helps to preserve the energy of the original sketch.

I love being able to work out composition problems on the computer, which can save hours of drawing and redrawing. However, all of my final art is entirely by hand, and I don't do 'blue-line pencils' as many artists do.

The Fair Lord is based on two works by Clarke: the main figure in *The Mad Mulrannies*, Clarke's illustration for JM Synge's *The Playboy of the Western World*, and his stained-glass work, *The Song of the Mad Prince*. *The Mad Mulrannies* was also the basis for the art on page 18. Other references from Clarke's art include illustrations from Poe's *The Pit and the Pendulum*, and a tiny spot illustration of two stylised horses ended up being incorporated into the queen's embroidery.

Clarke was the leader of the Irish Arts and Crafts Movement, and is probably best known for his stained glass. Since I'd only ever seen old, faded reproductions of his illustrations, Neil encouraged me to seek out his dazzling colour originals. I went to Dublin, Ireland to get photos and reproductions of many of Clarke's works featuring deep, jewel-like blues, which I incorporated into my colour approach, though my work is far more restrained than Clarke's.

I'm deeply grateful to Neil, our editor Daniel Chabon, and Dark Horse for giving me this great opportunity and so much creative freedom on this book.